The Basic Essentials of
SURVIVAL

by James Churchill

**Illustrations by
Scott Power**

ICS BOOKS, Inc.
Merrillville, Indiana

THE BASIC ESSENTIALS OF SURVIVAL

Copyright © 1989 by James Churchill

10 9 8 7 6 5 4 3

Printed in U.S.A.

Published by:
ICS Books, Inc.
One Tower Plaza
107 E. 89th Avenue
Merrillville, IN 46410

Library of Congress Cataloging-in-Publication Data

Churchill, James E., 1934-
    Survival : the basic essentials of / by James E. Churchill ;
illustrations by Scott Power.
      p.   cm. -- (The Basic essentials series)
    ISBN 0-934802-48-3
    1. Wilderness survival.   I. Title   II. Title: Basic essentials
of survival.
GV200.5.C48   1989
613.6'9--dc20
                                       89-36794
                                          CIP

TABLE OF CONTENTS

INTRODUCTION

This book is a basic guide to the skills you might need if suddenly stranded, whether in the deep wilderness or only a few miles from home. But, far more important than any book or device is your reasoning ability and attitude.

The Creator gave us the ability to overcome any challenge. But, when faced with danger we must stay calm and allow the reasoning process to develop. And never give up. Always keep trying. The worst challenge you will ever face has probably been overcome by someone before. People have endured incredible deprivation and lived to tell about it.

But, the object of this book is to outline the skills and tell what action should be taken so you don't have to ever see how much misery you can endure. Never go into territory without knowing which way you must go to get out. Always carry a compass and learn how to use it. Always dress for the worst conditions you might encounter and carry a basic survival kit. Finally, make sure someone knows where you have gone so searchers know where to start looking for you.

Learn how to make a fire with natural materials and build a shelter from the forest or plains. Learn to catch animals and fish and find edible wild plants and prepare them.

Almost anything can be made from the natural objects if you have the skill. I once watched John Sinclair make an excellent stone knife from the stones and shrubs growing around our cabin in northern Wisconsin. I am still using this stone knife four years later for certain projects. Develop your skills and knowledge beforehand and getting stranded may be more interesting than exhausting.

Also, learn to utilize what you have along. For instance, a bright colored sleeping bag waved aloft is a noticeable signaling device and the cosmetic mirror you have along can be used to reflect sunlight into the cabin of an aircraft to alert the pilot.

Good reading.

1. MAKING A FIRE

No one should go into a wilderness area without some means of starting a fire. I carry a plastic 35mm film container full of stick matches. I break them off to fit, but this small container will hold two dozen matches if the ends are alternated. It can be carried in any pocket and will keep the matches dry even if I fall in the water. I have several of these containers, and recently one appeared that had been in a coat pocket for a year. The matches still worked perfectly.

Waterproof camping matches are available from camping supply outlets, or you can make your own by coating kitchen matches with paraffin also.

An excellent fire starter for survivors is a device called a magnesium fire starter or "metal match." It consists of a block of magnesium and a flint insert. A small pile of magnesium is scraped from the block with a knife. Then the insert is scraped with the knife to produce fat, hot sparks that will ignite the magnesium. This device will work even if it gets wet, and the burning magnesium will ignite any dry tinder. A disposable cigarette lighter is also a good fire starter, and most will give more than 1,000 lights. They are light in weight and inexpensive and will work even after they get wet.

    People do get lost, however, and for one reason or another
have no fire making materials along, or they quickly use up their
supply of matches. Therefore, every outdoorsman should learn to
make a fire by primitive methods.

    The bow and drill method of starting a fire is the most versatile.
It should be learned by anyone that is at risk of getting lost or
stranded. The raw materials are at hand wherever trees grow. The
string for the bow can be made from a boot lace or even coated
wire from a vehicle wiring harness. This method is far from easy.
Don't wait until you are stranded to learn how to make a bow and
drill.

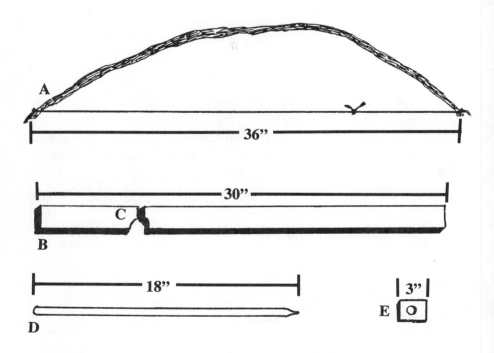

Figure 1
Bow and drill fire starter. The bow (A) should be 36" in length. The fire board
(B) should be 30" in length, however the fire hole (C) should be put in on the
flat side about 24" from a chosen end. The drill (D), 18" in length and the socket
(E), which hold the drill, 3" in width.

I spent about eight hours of concentrated activity before getting a fire burning from a bow and drill. But now that the device is made I can usually get a fire going in a half hour or so. A new hole has to be drilled in the fire board every two or three lights because the drill will wear out the original hole. The fire drill has to be reshaped quite often also.

Figure 2
Use the bow and drill to make a fire.

Here's how I made mine: Using a large belt knife, I split a three foot length of white spruce limb to make the fire board. It is about one inch thick and three inches wide. Next I found a dead seasoned maple sapling about 5/8 inch in diameter and shaped it into a fire drill eighteen inches long. The bottom end was tapered to about a 45 degree angle and the top of the drill was simply rounded off and made as smooth as possible. The drill headpiece was a dead, seasoned piece of maple log about three inches square. A socket was gouged into the center of the headpiece to fit the top end of the drill. I lubricated it with earwax and oil from beside my nose.

Working carefully I used the point of the knife to drill a hole in the fire board that would fit the taper on the fire drill. Directly underneath the hole a V shaped notch was formed to hold the tinder.

A hard maple limb with a natural bow shape made a 36 inch long bow. I used my boot laces for a bow string. Notches were cut near each end of the bow to keep the laces from slipping. The string has to be tied fairly snug but not tight since the the fire drill is wrapped in the string.

I placed the tapered point of the drill in the hole in the fire board, held the top with the headpiece and sawed the bow back and forth to spin the drill. The drill soon milled the hole to a snug fit and shortly thereafter smoke started coming from the hole. I stopped then and went looking for tinder.

I found a dead cedar tree and made tinder from the inner bark. It was shredded until it was so light and fluffy it would almost float in the air. The tinder was packed into the V notch under the hole in the fire board. Finally after several hours of drilling, reshaping the drill and its seat in the fire board and trying again, I got the tinder smoldering and blew it into a flame.

To sum up; this method of making a fire is far from easy or quick, but it definitely works. Best of all, the components can be built from natural materials and if no knife was at hand they probably could be made with a sharp rock or a piece of broken glass.

If you have a black powder firearm along, you can sometimes start a fire by ramming tinder down the barrel against the powder charge. Use charred cloth if available. Fire the gun up in the air, run and pick up the cloth and blow it into flame. Have a supply of tinder at hand so the cloth can be placed against it to start the fire.

Fires can be started with a magnifying glass also if the sun is nearly overhead and shining brightly. A small magnifying glass can be carried along on an expedition for just this purpose. I have a "bull's eye" magnifying glass that will start a fire in a minute or less when good tinder is available. But, with any type of magnifying glass the lens is moved back and forth until the sunlight shining through the glass is adjusted to a small brilliant dot. Situate the dot to shine on a tight ball of tinder and it will quickly start smoking. Hold the tinder in one hand and the magnifying glass in the other so you can blow on the tinder after it starts smoldering. This is not as easy as it might sound and you should practice this procedure beforehand.

Figure 3
A bulls eye magnifying glass and natural tinders will quickly start a fire.

A telephoto lens from a camera can be used to start a fire also. Remove the lens from the camera and use the same procedure as for the burning glass. Lenses taken from binoculars and telescopic rifle sights also can be put together to produce a magnifying glass to start a fire.

Figure 4
A telephoto lens and natural tinder will also start a fire.

A battery from a disabled vehicle or airplane can be used to quickly start a fire. Take it out of the vehicle if possible. Then tear out a two to three feet long piece of wire from the vehicle's wiring harness. Use headlight wiring or some other non- critical wiring if the vehicle might be used again. Strip both ends of the wire and wrap one end around the negative terminal of the battery. Then find a rag and soak it with gasoline. Loosen or break a fuel line if you can't dip the rag in the tank. Lay the gasoline soaked rag against the positive terminal. Then using gloves, touch the other end of the wire to the positive terminal. The rag will ignite instantly. Place the burning rag under some previously gathered tinder. No need to use fine tinder for this fire. Instead, good sized dead twigs can be set afire.

I have tried to get a fire burning without success from sparks made with flint and steel, from firing a gun fueled with smokeless, modern powder, with a fire plough and a fire thong. I don't believe they are a workable way for a survivor to get a fire burning even though they are recommended in many books.

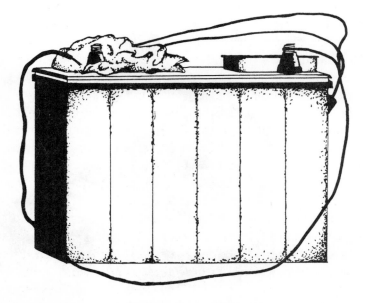

Figure 5
Start a fire with a battery and gasoline soaked rag. Use other tinder if no rags or gasoline are available.

Tinder

Regardless of the method used for making a fire, however, it won't be successful without good tinder. Learn to recognize this material before you get stranded. The inner bark from dead trees, dry small twigs shredded between the fingers, dead grass shredded between the fingers, mouse nests, downy feathers, wasps nests, dried evergreen needles, dry moss, cattail fluff, punky material from inside dead elderberry stalks, and dried animal dung will make good tinder.

If the surrounding forest is wet, finding dry tinder is more difficult. Try the wispy bark from birch trees that can be gathered without a knife. It is impregnated with oil and doesn't absorb moisture. The inner bark from dead standing trees, and the inner core of a rotting stump that can be kicked apart might have dry tinder. Don't forget the paper in your wallet, the cuffs of your shirt, your handkerchief or even the top of your shirt tail can be shredded to make tinder when the surrounding area is wet.

Firewood

Good tinder is very important to start the fire, but good dry fuel to keep it burning is equally needed. Be sure the fuel is piled so the tinder can be placed underneath it. Tiny dry twigs piled teepee fashion will quickly catch fire if placed over burning tinder. Have some larger twigs at hand to put on the fire. After branches an inch or so in diameter are burning, there will be time to gather larger fuel. Gradually increase the size until logs six inches or more in diameter will burn. They will hold a fire for hours. If they can't be cut up in short lengths, just push the ends into the fire, let them burn off and push up another length.

Sometimes fuzz sticks can be made up easier than finding small twigs. Take a short length of twig an inch or so in diameter and whittle it towards one end so a shaving is produced. But, don't cut the shaving off. Leave it on the branch so the end result looks like a shuttlecock. Lean the fuzz sticks against each other, teepee fashion, and place the burning tinder underneath them.

Most survival fires will be fueled with whatever wood is nearby. Seldom will you have a choice of woods to use. Soft woods, such as dry evergreen wood, burn fast and produce sparks, but often this is all you have. Dry aspen, dry alders and maple tree limbs all make very good wood that will last for hours. A fire will burn overnight if you lay two green logs across the burning campfire so that flames will come up between them. If they get a good start before the rest of the dry wood burns up, they will smolder along all night.

When it is difficult to get a fire burning, be sure it doesn't go out when you are sleeping or during a rainstorm. Always keep at least one coal alive. At night, bank the fire first with ashes and then a layer of dirt so the coals will stay alive. If it rains, cover the banked fire with bark, a flat stone, or whatever waterproof covering is at hand. When you move, carry a live coal in a tin can or bark container. Cover the coal with an inch thick layer of ashes and it will not burn the container or die for as long as 48 hours. Rotten but dry wood will hold a fire for a long time also without bursting into flame. It can be carried along and blown into flame when needed.

2. HOW TO FIND THE RIGHT DIRECTION

Last year near a small town in upper Michigan, a couple stopped at a motel. It was early in the afternoon and the elderly lady decided to go for a walk. She never returned. Weeks later a search party found her body beside a wood's road about twelve miles from the motel.

Even though it was summer, hypothermia set in after dark and she expired. Yet, if she had known the right direction she could have walked to help in a half hour.

We live on the edge of a large expanse of forest, and several times lost deer hunters have followed the light to our cabin after they got lost. Some are seasoned woodsmen. Most times they have no idea where their vehicle is and even after I find it for them they are so disoriented they don't know the way back to town until I tell them. Usually they are on the verge of exhaustion, and in the Wisconsin northwoods in winter an exhausted human might not last until morning.

I get turned around about as often as anyone and always have. But, knowing of this weakness I have trained myself to react wisely when I discover I am not walking the right direction. One good example happened in a western hunting trip.

I was tracking an elk on a mountainside near Pinedale, Wyoming, when I finally lost track of the herd. Then I realized that the peak I had absently been looking at from time was not the peak I thought it was.

I remember feeling in my pocket for the compass and the great feeling of utter joy and relief that came over me when my groping fingers touched it. With compass in hand, I plotted a course. At first I was tempted to walk due north, hoping to hit the horse trail. But, changed my mind when I thought how easy it would be to walk right beside the trail and never know it was there. I decided instead to walk east to a large burned over area. Then follow its edge to the north side of the peak and then walk west to the horse trail.

I had barely started walking when it began snowing heavily, almost blotting out the landscape. With no sun to guide me, the compass literally became a life saving device. At that I didn't reach the trail until just before dark. I could have easily died on that peak that night because after it stopped snowing it turned bitterly cold. The compass literally saved me.

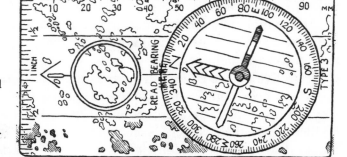

Figure 6
Every out-doorsman should know the basic fundamentals of using a compass.

No one should set out into unfamiliar territory without a compass. However, if you happen to be stranded in a polar region or in an exceptionally ore rich territory where compasses don't work properly, or if your compass is lost or damaged there are still several ways of determining the proper direction.

First, as most everyone knows the sun rises in the east and sets in the west. But, it neither rises in a due east direction or sets in a true west direction except in certain areas. In fact, in the far north the position of the sun can be very misleading, and so the stick and shadow method should be used to plot due east and west. Further, the stick and shadow method can sometimes be used on cloudy days when the sun isn't visible because even on a cloudy day the sun might cast a shadow. The moon also can be used if it is bright enough to cast a shadow.

Figure 7
Shadow sticks used for finding directions. The two shorter sticks lie in an East/West direction. The last stick to be put in will be East.

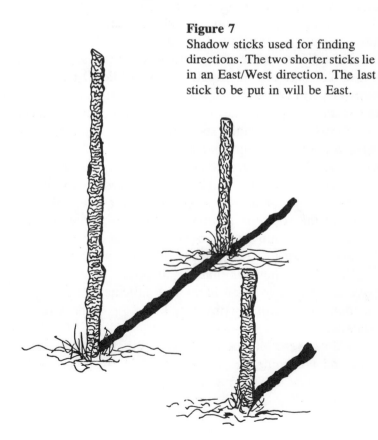

First, cut a stick at least three feet long and stick it upright in the ground where the ground is flat and bare of vegetation. Then cut two marker sticks about one foot long and stick one in the ground at the tip of the shadow cast by the three foot stick. About 1/2 hour later drive the second stick in the tip of the shadow again. It will have moved from the first mark. Now cut a direction pointer stick, sharpen one end, lay it against the two marker sticks with the sharp end against the second marker stick. The sharpened end will point east and the blunt end will point west. This will be true anywhere in the world since the sun always moves in an east to west path.

Now having marked true east and west, align your body with the direction stick so your extended right arm will point east and your left arm directly west. Now you will be facing north. With all four directions found, you can plot your travel path from them.

At night if the moon isn't shining enough to cast a shadow, and the stars are visible, find the North Star to determine north direction. This star is always located in the same position in the sky at the end of the handle of the Little Dipper. For practical purposes, the entire constellation Little Dipper is close enough to true north for short journeys with no pinpoint destination in mind.

Actually any bright star can be used for plotting directions. Drive a stick in the ground and then back off about ten feet and drive another in the ground so you can sight across the top of the two sticks at the star. If you watch the star for several minutes across the tops of the stick, it will either rise, fall, swing to the left or to the right. If it falls you are looking west, if it is rising you are sighted towards the east. Swinging towards the left you are looking north, towards the right will indicate south. But, you only have to remember that a rising star indicates east and a star moving towards your left hand will indicate you are sighting across the sticks in a northerly direction since the other two directions are opposite.

All of these methods of finding the directions should be practiced and committed to memory before an emergency develops. Then it will be second nature.

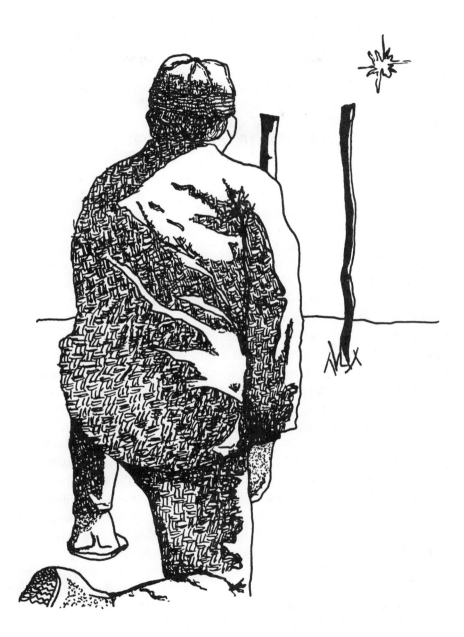

Figure 8
Sight across two sticks at a star. If it rises you are looking East. If it moves to the left you are looking North.

3. FINDING WATER

Water is easy to find on most of the remote places left on earth. The far north has snow and ice in winter and plenty of surface water in summer. Jungles are well watered, and many plains areas have rivers and potholes full of water.

Most of this surface water is contaminated and should be treated or boiled before it is ingested. Be sure to take water purifying tablets along if you will be flying over, or traveling through remote areas. But, if you don't have tablets, the water should be boiled at least ten minutes before being consumed. Only in a dire emergency should untreated surface water be consumed and then a doctor should be advised after you reach civilization again.

Desert and arid regions are a different matter. In the desert dying of thirst is a distinct possibility and every desert traveler should develop their water finding skills beforehand.

A man in the desert who did not exert himself could live from two to three days with temperatures 100 degrees or more without water. At 50 to 75 degrees a man without water can live up to ten days. In the desert an inactive person can live for five days if he has two quarts of water a day. On the same amount of water at 75 degrees he should live ten days. In cool temperatures a person can be mildly active and live on two quarts a day indefinitely.

Fortunately water is found nearly everywhere and even on the driest desert it sometimes can be located. If such dire emergency arose that you would have to try to walk out from the desert without water and no other destination, head for the roughest ground or for visible vegetation. If you can get to the hills there might be water near their base. A dry creek bed also might have water somewhere running underground. Palm trees, cattail grass, bushes and greasewood can grow only where water is found near the surface.

Animal trails probably lead to water in the desert and birds can point out a waterhole. They often circle over a water source, or their flight patterns are often directly towards water. Animals might scratch at the surface where water is close to the surface and sometimes honey bees or other insects will gather on moist ground.

If you have a piece of plastic along on your person or in the stranded vehicle or airplane, a solar still can be made. Dig a pit in the lowest land available, about two feet deep and three feet in diameter, or as large as your sheet of plastic will cover. Leave enough slack so you can place a rock in the center of the plastic to pull it down to a cone shape. But, the first step after digging the pit is to place a tin can, a shoe or hat or other object that will hold water at the center of the bowl. Now place the plastic across the top of the pit and hold it around the rim with sand or rock. If the ground around the pit holds any moisture it will evaporate out and condense on the plastic. Then it will run down the sides of the cone to drip into the container under the plastic.

Up to three pints of water a day can be extracted from some desert soils this way. Try to remove the plastic only once a day just before dark. If any other source of moisture is available, even the pulp, stems or leaves from plants, it can be placed under the plastic. The plant juice will evaporate and condense again into water also. A solar still can be used to convert swamp or alkali water to pure drinking water. Dig a trench under the plastic and fill it with the contaminated water.

When water is available, conserve it as much as possible by moving only during the coolest part of the day. Talk very little,

DESERT SOLOR STILL

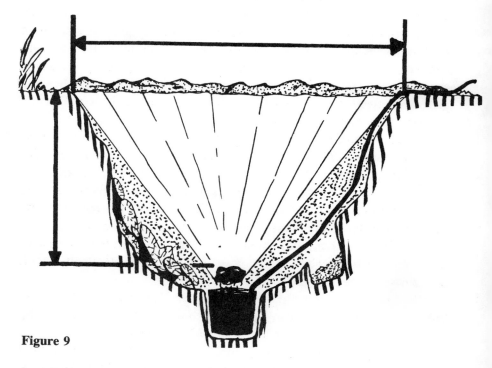

Figure 9

Legend:
1. Sheet of wettable plastic, 6 foot diameter.
2. Smooth, fist sized rock for forming cone of plastic.
3. Pail, jar, can, or cone of soil, plastic or canvas to catch water.
4. Drinking tube, 1/4 inch plastic, about 5 feet long.
   (Desirable but not necessary.)
5. Soil to weight plastic sheet and seal space. A good closure is important.
6. Line hole with broken cacti or other succulents.
7. If non-potable water is available, dig a soaking trough around inside of
   hole. Carefully fill the trough to prevent impure water from running
   down and contaminating the water-catching container.

don't smoke or eat unless the food is also full of moisture. Breathe through the nose and keep your clothing on since this will cut down the rate of perspiration somewhat. When you rest in the shade, try to make a bed about a foot above the sand. It can be 30 degrees cooler a foot above the ground. If you can't rest above the ground, dig down into the sand about two feet.

The human body can store water for short periods also to some extent. Drink all the water you can before you set out on an arid journey. It is possible to saturate the tissues enough so you can go a day or two without serious dehydration. Some travelers place a pebble or two in their mouths to keep the saliva flowing so the mouth doesn't feel too dry.

Watch also for water holes built in extremely remote locations for desert sheep. They are called guzzlers. Aalso, if you are lucky you might spot a windmill, or cattle or sheep watering pond.

Prickly pear cactus grows in great quantities and the pad and fruit both contain large amounts of juice. Try not to get scratched as the thorns are long and wicked. Also, the stakes of mescal, sotol, Spanish bayonet and barrel cactus all can be cut and drained of their juices for emergency use. Cut the pulp into pieces and suck on them.

Collect rain water in hollows in the ground coated with plastic or cloth. Sop up water from puddles with clothing or handkerchiefs. Quickly dam up any nearby trenches to form pools.

Dew can be heavy even on the desert sometimes. It will collect on stones, vegetation or metal surfaces such as auto bodies or airplane wings. Mop it up with a cloth and squeeze out into a container. If there are nearby trees, the dew collects on the surface of the leaves. Mop it up also. When tall grass or brush is wet with dew, tie rags around your ankles and walk through the dew soaked vegetation. Wring out the rags in a container afterwards.

In arid regions where grass is growing and has been growing for many years atop rocks, there will be a layer of muck or mud below the grass. Dig into this muck to look for water. There might be water just underground. Dig out the earth filler in cracks and let the water run out.

In arid regions keep an eye out for cottonwood trees. Find the largest cottonwoods. They are almost a sure indicator of water. Dig in any nearby low places for water. Where white brush grows is a sure indicator of water, where mesquite grows will probably be a dry area.

Streams, rivers and lakes flow in great profusion in most northern and mountainous areas, and water usually can be found without much trouble. If possible, it should be boiled for ten minutes. Water, even in remote places, can be contaminated with a half dozen diseases that are carried by animals. But, if a spring can be found that bubbles up from the ground, the water will probably be pure.

Stagnant water, even if it is badly contaminated with algae or mud, can be made potable by straining it through a filter made by tying a trouser leg at the bottom, partially filling the leg full of clean sand and then pouring the water into the leg so it must run through the sand. Catch it in a container. It also should be boiled before drinking. Several layers of cloth will also strain most particles of contamination from the water, and sometimes you can dig a hole into the bank a few yards inland from the shore of a pond and find water that is clean. It also should be boiled if possible.

Sometimes a vessel can be hollowed out of wood, or a bowl shaped stone can be found that will hold enough water to boil. Of course, if you have no choice, drink the cleanest, coldest water you can find.

It is possible that you will be caught along a sea coast in a survival situation without fresh water. Often water can be found that is drinkable back away from the sea coast by digging into the sand. If you don't dig too deep the slightly salty water is palatable. Dig mud holes to catch rain water.

Where snow and ice are present, no one will die of thirst. Eat snow if you can't melt it. Melt it only if you have a plentiful supply of fuel. It takes ten inches of snow to make an inch of water. Eating snow and ice will not make your mouth sore if you only eat small amounts at one time.

4. FINDING FOOD

Starving to death is not an immediate problem. Most of us can go weeks without eating if necessary. In fact, for many people after about three days the sensation of hunger leaves and doesn't return for a week or more. But, food is an important morale builder as well as fuel for the muscles and brain, and as soon as adequate shelter is constructed most people will start looking for sustenance.

If you are stranded along a watercourse fish can be caught by hook and line, speared or caught in traps.
Fish hooks can be fashioned from twigs, fish skeltons, small animal bones or thorns. A gorge type fish hook can be made by just sharpening a small twig on each end. Make a groove at the center for fastening the line.

Fish line is somewhat harder to obtain. Some clothing can be unraveled enough to produce a fish line. A leather belt can be cut into thin laces and used for fish line and the inner bark of some trees is strong enough to make a fish line when cut into strips and knotted together. Wire from a vehicle or airplane also might be used for fish line.

19

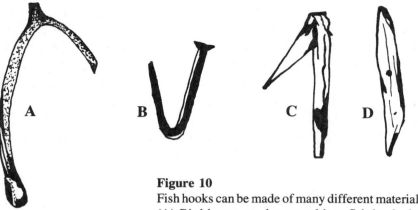

Figure 10
Fish hooks can be made of many different materials.
(A) Bird bones can be carved into fish hook shape.
(B) A bent nail. (C) Fish hook made from a thorn.
(D) A gorge made from a branch.

A fish spear can be made from forest materials. We made spears for spearing suckers when I was young by just cutting a green hardwood sapling about eight feet long and two inches in diameter. On the lowest end cut a V notch in the end and sharpen both points very well. Barbs are not necessary on a survival type fish spear because the fish is speared and then held to the bottom of the lake until you can reach down and grab it with your hands. A crotched stick also can be used to pin fish to the bottom where the bottom is firm.

Figure 11
(A) Crotched stick and (B) carved hand spear both to catch fish.

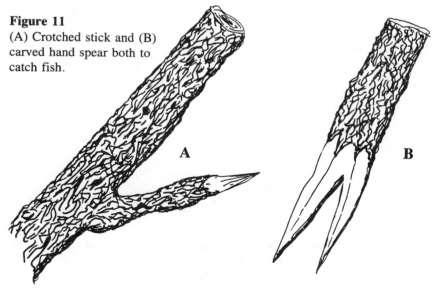

After the spear is made, position yourself on a rock or log overlooking the shallows and stay as still as possible. When a fish comes into view, slowly slide the spear into the water. Get as close to the fish as you can without actually touching it. Aim low to allow for refraction of the water and then make a hard thrust.

If you arrange to make a torch, try night spearing. Some fish are actually attracted to light and others just ignore it. At night they are often in shallow water feeding and offer good targets. Fish also can be clubbed when they are in very shallow water or killed by dropping stones on them.

Be sure to put out a few fish traps also. The traps can be made from rocks or with stakes pounded into the bottom of the lake. The shallow water section of a shoreline point is a good location for the traps, as is the inlet or outlet from the lake. These traps work well in streams also. Sometimes fish can be driven downstream into the trap.

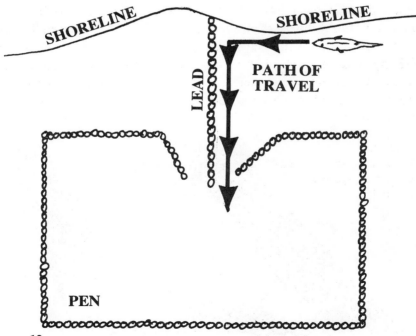

Figure 12
Fish move along the shoreline after dark. When they encounter the lead, they turn towards deep water and are confined in the pen. Use logs or stones for the lead and pen. They have to project above the waterline. The lead should be about ten feet long if possible. The pen as large as you can make it.

Minnows are very abundant in most lakes, streams and rivers. Often they will supply more pounds of food than larger fish, since they are much easier to get. Make a minnow trap by finding a hollow driftwood log, one to three feet long. Close off one end with branches or rocks. Then put fish guts or other bait in the end of the log nearest the branches. Place the log where you have seen minnows in the shallows and weight it down with rocks so it sinks. Then find a birch tree or other type of tree with peelable bark and remove a section about 15 inches x 20 inches and roll it into a funnel. The small end of the funnel should be about two inches in diameter. Push the funnel into the log with the small end inward. A few such traps placed in good locations can catch two to ten pounds of minnow a day.

Strip the waste matter from their intestines by squeezing them and then swallow them whole. They can be eaten raw or baked on a hot rock.

Larger fish can be snared if you have some light wire or string along. Make a noose in the line and when you see a resting fish,

Figure 13
Minnow and small fish trap.

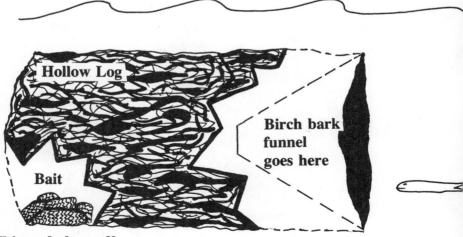

This end close off.

approach it very carefully and work the noose over its head, back of the gills. Then jerk it quickly.

Some fish can be grabbed by hand if you move slowly until your hand is under their belly. Then throw them out on the bank or grab them in the gills.

Figure 14
Pounds of minnows can be caught with a net from a jacket in one scoop. Minnows can keep you from starving to death when big fish are hard to catch.

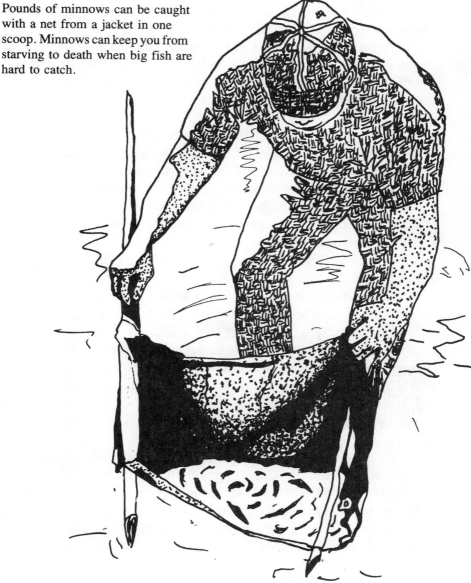

Watch eagles and hawks also. Sometimes you might be able to scare them away from their kill of a large fish.

In winter, chop a hole in the ice and make a sharp gaff whittled from a tree branch to gig fish when they swim under the hole in the ice. Leave the gaff in the water until the fish is positioned directly above the hook. Then jerk it upwards to drive the point of the gaff into the fish's belly. Keep lifting it to bring the fish up through the hole in the ice. A wooden gaff can also be used to catch fish from open water.

In many places rabbits and squirrels along with gophers and chipmunks, porcupine, skunks, marmot and other small animals can be harvested by many different methods. Grouse, ducks, geese, crows, gulls and all the birds of prey are edible, as well as small song birds.

Gophers and ground squirrels, tree squirrels and cottontail rabbits can be found in ground burrows or in hollow trees. Where the ground is soft you can dig the animals out with a sharp stick used as a shovel. If some means of carrying water is at hand you can pour water down the burrow until you drown the animal out. If you reach the animal with a stick, make a twisting stick from a forked tree branch. Push the stick against the animal and turn it to wind up the hair. Then pull the animal out where you can kill him with another club.

The most efficient, easiest to make and position is the snare. Snares can be used to catch everything from a mouse to a moose. A snare is simply a noose that will tighten over an animal's or bird's body when it tries to go through it. A noose can be made from your belt or your shoe laces to snare small animals. But, if soft wire is at hand, by all means use it since it will make a fine snare. Strong fish line also can be used for a snare. If heavy cable or several strands of heavy wire can be found, a snare can be made that will catch deer or a small moose.

Use a snare four inches in diameter, set about two inches from the ground for rabbits. About eighteen inches in diameter, set two feet above the ground for deer or moose. Learn to use a snare before you get stranded by reading fur animal trapping books.

Set the snare in a runway where animals have made a distinct path. These runs are easy to find on the snow, but somewhat harder

Figure 15
If you have the material make up from 40 to 100 snares to set around your camp.
It will require this many to keep you in food, especially during summer when
animals do not follow trails most of the time.

in summer. Look for small paths through clumps of thick berry vines or underbrush.

You can also snare birds and animals by pulling on a noose when they are in the right position. Prop up the snare, attach a long cord and conceal yourself nearby. When the animal or bird is in the right position, pull it tight.

Make a box trap from forest materials. The trap is made so when the animal enters to get the bait a door will fall down behind it and confine it to the box.

A box trap can be made of logs or stakes. Cut stakes about eighteen inches long and sharpen one end. Drive them into the

Figure 16
Snowshoe hares are fairly easy to catch when traps are widespread and plentiful. However, never underestimate the difficulty of catching animals.

ground about an inch apart to form a rectangle ten inches wide and eighteen inches long. Close off one end and roof the tops with a log or with several smaller poles tied to the sidewalls.

The open end will be fitted with a door also made from materials at the site. The door must slide up and down in the four end stakes of the sidewalls. Tie a string to the top of the door and run it to the back of the trap. Fit this end with a trigger that will hold the door up when the string is tight, but drop it when the animal bites on the bait. See accompanying illustration.

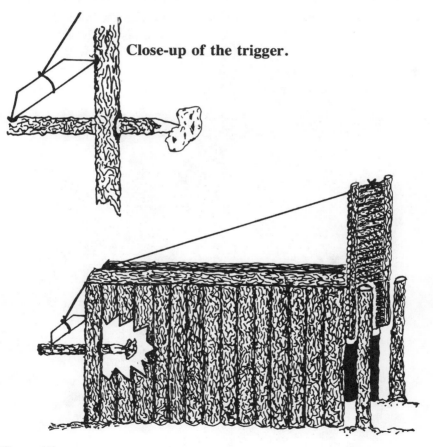

Close-up of the trigger.

Figure 17

The animal enters the trap and bites the bait. This moves the bait stick and the trigger slips out of its notch, releasing the string. The door falls, trapping the animal inside. This trap will have to be watched closely. The animal will dig or gnaw out in a short time.

Finding bait for the trap can be difficult. Small animals usually have plenty of food, but they crave salt, and you can produce a salt bait from your own urine. First find a porous piece of wood small enough to be used as a bait for a box trap. Place the piece of wood on a small bowl shaped depression in a rock that will hold liquid. Urinate on this piece of wood exclusively so the wood is soaking in urine. The salt in your urine will impregnate the wood and after a few days it will be salty enough to attract small animals. Fasten the piece of wood to the trigger of the trap.

If you are trying to survive in the forested regions of North America, look for a beaver pond. Beaver populations have exploded until their ponds dot almost all wilderness areas. One large beaver can feed a man for days. Moreover, their ponds will certainly contain fish, clams, crayfish, and frogs, as well as be a watering hole for nearby deer or moose, which also can be used for food.

Figure 18
Beaver can definitely keep you from starving. Find a colony and trap, snare, club or spear them. A good sized beaver will weigh 50 pounds.

You can get a beaver with a club. First look along the edges for signs of beaver cuttings, if you see a tree that is partly cut off and the cutting looks like it is free,the beaver will probably return to finish cutting it off that evening. Make a blind from tree branches or whatever is at hand and wait for the beaver to come out of the water. Be sure you are downwind from the animal and have a stout heavy club. Beaver have strong skulls and bodies and it takes a tremendous wallop to disable one. Wait until it is clear of the water, get between it and the pond and run it down. Beaver cannot move very fast on land.

If they won't come out on the bank, find the weakest part of the dam and pull it apart. A tremendous sluice of water will gush out. Stand by it with a club to kill any fish or muskrats that might ride this spillway out of the pond.

Long before the water is all out of the dam the beaver will turn out to try and repair it. They will swim up to the hole in the dam and examine it. Then they will disappear and return shortly with material to start fixing it. Hide nearby with a club or spear. If you don't get them this way, wait until the water is low enough so you can wade out to the beaver's lodge. Chase the beaver out of the lodge by pushing a stick down into the lodge through the air hole opening in the top of the lodge. When they come out, have a club or spear ready. They also might swim out to earth dens in the banks where they can be dug out. Beaver can be snared also if you have some stout wire along.

In the spring and early summer the young beaver will not come out. But, they will start mewing when the old ones leave. If you hear this sound, tear the lodge apart and get them. They will be at least as big as rabbits and are excellant eating. These methods are illegal in most states, but if your life is in danger they must be used.

In the far north in the spring of the year, look for a wetland where ducks and geese may be nesting. The eggs, young birds and also the adult birds might be easy to get because you can catch the birds on the nest. Adult geese are respectable adversaries and could even break your arm unless you are armed with a stout club. They also can bite hard enough to draw blood.

When waterfowl are roosting in large flocks, you should be able to kill one or two by throwing a club into their midst. Also, if you happen to find the waterfowl during the moulting season, they cannot fly. They can be run down and dispatched.

In remote areas Franklin's grouse, spruce grouse and ruffed grouse are unwary enough so you can get close enough to them to kill them with a club. In the spring watch on the ground at the base of a clump of willows or the base of a tree for grouse and ptarmigans nest also. You might be able to get both the hen and her eggs.

According to records, would-be survivors have starved to death from what might be called "plate fright". They just couldn't eat what was available to them. Human beings can digest insects, snakes, lizards, grubs found under tree bark and most other creatures that move about on the earth. Don't turn down any food in a suvival situation. In early morning, earthworms can sometimes be found on top of the ground. Squeeze them so they expel the contents of their innards and eat raw or baked on a hot rock.

Don't forget the hundreds of edible green plants also. Most plants are edible, but a few are poisonous. Don't eat mushrooms or any plant with a milky sap, otherwise most every other plant is edible if not palatable. Even the buds and the inner bark from trees are edible, as is cattail roots, acorns and cactus fruits.

Be sure to learn how to find and prepare edible wild plants and how to catch animals and fish before you are stranded.

5. MAKE A SURVIVAL CAMP

In all but a few instances the most self serving procedure is to make a bivouac camp and stay put after you realize you are lost. Transportation is so rapid and search efforts are so intense and well executed in this modern age it is nearly always senseless to move. Spend you energy improving your camp, putting out signaling devices and finding food.

In the northern regions the evergreen trees are the best friend a lost man ever had. Their thick boughs can be used to make a warm comfortable bed and to cover a pole framework to make a shelter. Moreover, the air temperature under a thick stand of evergreens is actually up to ten degrees higher than in open areas. Further, the thick treee usually break the wind which considerably reduces the chill factor caused by moving air.

Therefore, if you are forced to spend the night in the woods in cold weather, by all means go into the thickest evergreen stand you can find to make your survival camp. If you have a knife or hatchet the work will be much easier, but limbs can be broken by hand. Especially in cold weather, limbs will readily snap off.

Figure 19
Build a pole and evergreen bough shelter starting with a broken-off tree. Such
a shelter can be built without tools by breaking the branches off.

Figure 20
Cover a pole frame
with pine boughs.
When done with
care such a shelter
can be made
almost wind proof.

There are downed trees in every forest. Find one that has broken off a few feet above the ground but has not separated from the stump. Break off the branches on the underside of the trunk so it will form a ridge pole. Leave the side branches attached and bring in the others to make a tent shaped framework. Cover this framework with evergreen boughs woven tightly together, make a bed of evergreen boughs and you have a dandy shelter that will withstand snow and wind. Also, put a six inch layer of pine boughs on the ground inside the shelter for a bed.

For a quick overnight shelter, look for a spruce or pine tree with limbs growing nearly to the ground. Break off the branches on the downwind side of the tree to make an opening large enough so you can sit with your back against the tree. Weave the branches that you cut off into the other branches to make it even tighter then it is naturally.

Also, put a thick layer of boughs on the ground to sit on so the moisture and cold from the ground will not reach your hips and legs. You can rest fully clothed in such a shelter during the dark hours. Practice building these shelters before you get lost. Then it will be an automatic task.

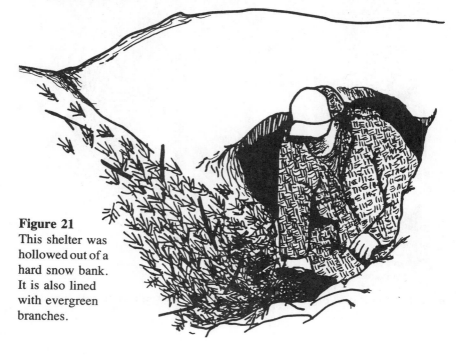

Figure 21
This shelter was hollowed out of a hard snow bank. It is also lined with evergreen branches.

In the plains or Arctic regions you may get caught in open country with night coming on and a blizzard blowing up. Immediately look for whatever natural shelter is available. Find the lee side of a ridge, a gulley or the downwind side of a huge boulder and make a shelter from the snow. If it is extremely cold, just dig into the snow. Use your hands and feet to scoop out a burrow. If possible, dig away the snow until you get to the earth underneath it.

If there is vegetation available to line the burrow, it will help keep your clothing dry. Logs or sticks, even though they will be uncomfortable to lie on will keep your clothing drier than lying in the snow.

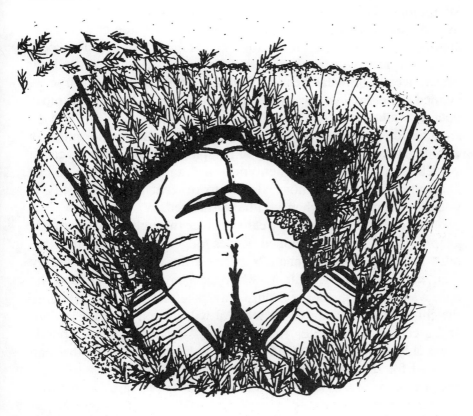

Figure 22
A trench shelter will keep you from freezing to death, but be careful not to work up a sweat making it.

If no natural windbreak is at hand, make a trench shelter in the snow. I have made these shelters using just my feet for a digging tool. I make them about eight feet long and three feet wide. They are formed at right angles to the wind so the sides of the trench break the wind. If grass, cattails, sage brush or evergreen boughs can be obtained to make a bed in the shelter it will positively keep you from freezing to death. Also, if available, find enough vegetation to put a roof over the trench. Then the blowing snow will cover the top and make it even warmer. If you can't cover the top, push the snow you removed from the trench into a ridge at least six feet upwind from the trench. This will act as a snow fence and keep most of the drifting snow from blowing into the hole.

A large fallen log or rock pile can form one side of a survival shelter also. Lay poles on the log or rocks to form a lean-to roof. Cover the roof with evergreen boughs, grass, sage brush, willow brush, weeds or whatever is available. Make it only as large as needed. The smaller the shelter the warmer it will be if no other heat is available except body heat.

Building a survival shelter is quite strenuous work, and it is easy to try to move so fast that you perspire heavily. This can cause your body to chill badly when you finish and stop moving about. Discipline yourself to move slowly to prevent this, especially if you can't start a fire when you have finished.

If you are following a stream or river through the wilderness, keep an eye out for abandoned beaver lodges. Sometimes they are built far from the main channel because the area was flooded by their dam when they built it. After the beaver have left and the dam washed out, the beaver house may be left high and dry. Enlarge the entrance so you can get in it and it will form a completely tight and weatherproof shelter for sleeping. Abandoned beaver ponds invariably have a good stand of dead poles lying around that can be used for shelter frames or for burning also.

In plains areas, sage brush sometimes grows large and sturdy enough to use as materials for making a shelter. Usually the densest growth is in gulleys and ravines where the sides of the gulley will also help break the wind and make the shelter more snug. If the stalks of the sage brush are not sturdy enough to use for a frame, pile rocks or dirt clods to form a trench shape high enough so you can sit or lie down in it. Pile sage brush around and over it to form a roof and sides.

Keep an eye out for a cave or overhanging bank in plains or mountainous or hilly terrain. A cave makes an excellent shelter, as will a partial cave if the sides can be covered with nearby tree branches or other vegetation.

Although Eskimos lived in igloos in the harshest climate on the globe, they are not survival shelters. It is far quicker and easier just to burrow into a hard snow bank for the shelter than to make an igloo unless you have the skill and tools.

A great many people are stranded in their cars each year during blizzards or because they were stuck in the sand or mud. Almost everybody that dies from such an incident left the vehicle and struck out on foot. Sometimes they had no clear idea of where they were going. It is far better to stay with your vehicle in nearly all instances.

When it is cold, keep warm by running the engine periodically, but be sure the exhaust pipe is not plugged by snow or mud, and also, keep a window open a crack so you won't be overcome by carbon monoxide poisoning.

After you run out of gas you might keep warmer outside the car because the metal body of an automobile conducts heat away very rapidly. You will need a wind tight shelter to survive very long in cold weather. Often there are materials or clothing in the car that can be used to make a lean-to type shelter. Floor mats, seat covers, trunk liners, seats, hood or trunk doors can be removed and used as part of the shelter. A warm bed can be made by using the cushions from the front and rear seats. Cut each one open and remove most of the stuffing material. The hollow formed will fit the human body. The foam material removed can be used to plug up drafty holes in the shelter. Nearby trees, brush, fence posts or road signs can be used to make sides for a shelter. If you can survive for three or four days, help will surely arrive.

People have expired after their car was stuck in the sand in the desert. Usually they died of thirst and heat prostration after they left their vehicle and tried to walk out. It is far better to stay with the vehicle. Sleep inside the car at night and burrow under the car into the sand during the daytime. Conserve your water supply by not sweating. If you work on the vehicle to try to get it unstuck, do this at night or in late afternoon or early morning. Don't move anymore then you have to during the heat of the day.

A large boulder, overhanging bank, dry stream bed or even the shady side of a cactus can be used to shelter yourself from the sun. If you can't find shade, try to lay or sit on some object several inches above the sand because it will be as much as twenty degrees cooler than the surface of the sand.

Small airplanes have been forced to land in the desert also. During the hot part of the day the airplane will be too warm to stay in. However, the fuselage and wings will create shade and this can be enhanced by using plastic or cloth material from the airplane draped over the wings to make a lean-to to turn the sun's rays. Digging into the sand even in the shelter will help the survivor stay cool. At night the interior of the airplane is an excellent shelter which will be safe from intrusion by poisonous snakes.

In cold climates the interior of the airplane is nearly the worst possible shelter since it will conduct heat away so rapidly. It will be mandatory to make a shelter outside the plane to avoid freezing to death. However, most airplanes that fly in the far north carry survival items along. A survival kit will usually include a tent or plastic tarp to use as a tent, space blankets, matches, flares, fishline and hooks and dried food. A parachute can be used to make a lean-to shelter or ground cloth.

If no survival materials have been carried along, fashion a shelter from the available natural materials as explained. The gasoline and oil and battery can be used to make a fire and for signaling.

6. SIGNALING FOR HELP

No one should go into remote territory without leaving word of where they are going and when they are expected back. If you walk out, leave a note in the vehicle when you are expected back. If you fly, be sure to file a flight report. Boaters also can leave word at a boat landing or with any available person.

Several devices are available for signaling in an emergency. A well equipped survival kit will include a flare gun and flares, as well as a signaling mirror and whistle.

Many survival kits also contain colored dye or colored cloth that can be laid out to make signals.

A great many people have been lost without any survival kit to aid them. They must improvise. Fire is the most noticeable signal that a survivor has at his disposal. The flame from fire is readily visible at night.

But, be sure to build the fire where it can be seen. On an island, on a lakeshore, on a hilltop, in a large clearing, or even on a floating log or raft out in the lake.

Smoke can be seen for many miles in the daytime and most of the forested regions of North America are watched over by men in fire spotting towers or by regular flights of airplanes whenever the ground is snow free. A fire six feet in diameter, well smothered with green boughs, grass or water plants will give off enough smoke to be spotted by fire spotters or searchers. Then help will arrive in a hurry.

If you can't keep a fire going continuously, lay the fire with tinder and fuel wood, cover it with birch bark or whatever is available to keep it from getting damp. Then when an airplane is heard, light the fire. Three large fires spaced 100 feet apart in a triangular shape will signal an airplane that you need help.

Many times an isolated dead tree standing in a clearing or along a lakeshore can be used as a signal tree. If the tree has dead branches so that it will burn well, pile grass, small dead branches or dried moss in the bottom limbs and have it ready to set a fire. The flames will climb up the tree and make a torch visible for many miles. Again the best time to light it is after an aircraft is heard.

Fire can be used to blacken a clearing, burn off a small island or blacken tree trunks or rocks to make a signal to searchers. Anything you can do to the surroundings to indicate that man has been present will attract a search plane. After an airplane has spotted you, smoke will show the pilot what direction the wind is blowing so he will know how to approach the landing. If possible, have a landing site picked out and marked.

When you are signaling from a disabled plane or vehicle, don't forget that a tire will make very dark smoke when it burns. Also, the oil from the engine will give off dark smoke when it burns, as well as being a good fire spotter. Gasoline is, of course, an excellent fire starter, but a spark can ignite the gasoline before it is needed. Tragic accidents have occurred when gasoline was thrown on a flame or on coals, so be careful. If you can mix the gasoline and oil together it will be less hazardous for starting the fire and will burn longer after it starts.

Signal mirrors also can be contrived from the materials at hand. A piece of broken glass covered on one side with dark mud will make a usable mirror. A tin can lid can be polished until it is like a mirror, a log slab kept wet from a nearby puddle can be used

Figure 23
A piece of wood
kept wet will
reflect light and
can be used for a
signaling device.

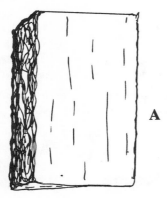
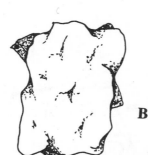
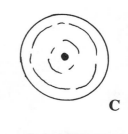

Figure 24
Signaling devices: (A) Piece of wood shaved
bright and kept wet. (B) A bright colored cloth.
(C) A tin can lid with a hole in the center, and
(D) a broken piece of glass covered with mud.   **D**

as a mirror to reflect light towards an overhead airplane. In winter
a slab of ice can be used for a mirror. Keep the mirror moving so
it will attract the pilot's attention.

When snow covers the ground, stamp out the letters SOS, fill
the letters with pine boughs or other dark materials. Make the letters
at least twenty feet high if you can. Letters laid out in a general
east-west pattern will cast a shadow and be much more visible from
the air.

If a tool is at hand to remove the bark from trees, peel several
trees in a group since this will make an eye catching signal from
the land or air. Rocks or logs piled in the pattern of a cross will
also attract attention. Make the cross about twenty to thirty feet
long, if possible.

If you have some bright colored clothing that can be spared,
climb a tree and tie it in the top where it will wave in the wind.
Waving bright colored paper or clothing with your hands will also
attract attention. At night torches waved around in the air are very
noticeable.

Shooting also can attract attention if done at the right time.
Wait until after dark when the hunting has ended for the day and
fire three evenly spaced shots. This is the universal distress signal.
Then stay quiet and wait for answering shots or shouts. If you get

Figure 25
Waving a bright colored jacket on the end of stick will catch a pilot's eye. This is also good in the mountains to signal land searchers.

Figure 26
A piece of glass coated with
mud works very well as a
signaling mirror and can be
sighted like a commercial
signaling mirror.

an answer, walk towards the sounds. But, if you don't hear any
more answers and it looks like you can't walk out, stop and stay
in one place until help arrives, or until the next morning.

In deep wilderness shooting isn't likely to attract attention and
will only waste the ammunition you might need to get food. The
exception would be after a search party was looking for you and
was close enough so you would hear them.

Whistling can attract attention and can be kept up longer than
shouting. A commercial whistle makes the most noise, but many
people can "shepherd whistle" also. Do this by placing the thumb
and forefinger together in the roof of the mouth. Then blow a quick
puff of air. This will make a sound almost as loud as a commercial
whistle.

Figure 27
Be sure to learn this hand signal which means "I need help." All pilots will recognize this signal. Do not just hold one hand up because that means, "I don't need help."

Pounding on a hollow log, on a rock, or any metal object, of course, will make considerable noise and this can be kept up for a long time to guide any nearby rescuers.

Signaling for help is largely a matter of common sense. Keep a clear head and utilize whatever materials are available. The first day or two that you are lost, sound signals will likely be the most effective. After that, an aircraft search will likely be initiated. Then sight signals are most apt to be spotted.

Be sure to learn the hand signal for communicating with an airplane pilot that means "I need help." The distress or "I need help" signal is to hold both hands above your head. Don't hold up just one hand since this means "I don't need help."

Above all, keep a clear head, make your camp or trail as visible as possible and make as much noise or light as possible. Do this and without a doubt you will soon be rescued.

7. WALKING OUT

Death, mental or physical illness, or just plain forgetfulness might cause a person to be stranded in a remote area without any means back home. Walking out might be mandatory.

But, before you start walking, ask yourself a few questions. Are you physically able to walk out? Can you make snowshoes or fashion skis to get through the deep snow? Do you have adequate clothing? Can you withstand the insects? Can you find food or water? Do you know the way?

After you decide to walk out, take your time deciding what to to take along. If you have a choice between taking a sleeping bag or shelter, take the shelter. You can sleep in your clothes. The tent will keep you from getting wet, with possible fatal complications in cold weather.

Matches or some fire starting device should not be overlooked. If a candle can be found, they are excellent for starting fires besides fulfilling their intended task of giving off some light. By all means take along spare socks if available. Don't forget a knife or hatchet.

Figure 28
Carry your clothes over your shoulder tied to a stick.

If no packsack is available, tie up the the items in a piece of cloth or canvas and sling it over your shoulder like the depression-era hobos did.

First line up some landmark. In heavily timbered country, this can be a faraway bluff, a lake, an exceptionally large tree or rocky outcrop. It often is impossible to walk directly to a landmark. You may have to skirt swamps or go around lakes. To keep from getting off the trail, sight on some close-by object such as a tree. Walk to it, then pick out another and walk to it. If this is done carefully you will get back to your original route without losing track of it.

When the sun is shining, of course, it will indicate the general direction. Walking directly into the rising sun will take you in an easterly direction, directly into the setting sun in a westerly direction, and if you want to walk east during the middle of the day, the sun should be over your right shoulder; a westerly route will be traveled if the sun is over your left shoulder. Walk south and the noonday sun will be shining in your face.

Night travel is an option in some areas. The insects might be so bad at night that you can't sleep and elect to travel. During the full or nearly full moon, this is quite possible even in wilderness territory. On the desert this might be the best time to travel to escape the hot sun.

The moon also rises in the east and sets in the west, so it will indicate the direction to travel. But, actual travel routes will still have to be determined by lining up objects and walking to them. Most nights you can't see very far ahead and must use nearby landmarks. It would, of course, be very foolish to travel in strange, rugged territory on a dark night. When traveling at night if you stop to rest, make a pointer to show where you came from and where you were going. Otherwise the next morning you may have forgotten which tree or landmark you were walking towards, or even which direction you were going.

Of course, no one should go into strange territory without a compass, and at least a rudimentary idea of how to use it. Know also in which direction the broadest target is likely to be found. A road or large settlement would be a much wiser goal to aim at than an outpost, even though the outpost is much closer.

For instance, imagine that you are lost in the deep forest east

Figure 29
Stop early enough to make camp and cook food to keep up your strength.

of Red Lake, Ontario, Canada. You know that Highway 105 lies west and offers broad lines to strike out for. This is nearly 40 miles away and will probably take you five to eight days since you will have to skirt numerous lakes. You also know that an outpost is located at Cat Lake only about ten miles away, and another outpost is found at Slate Falls, about fifteen miles distance. The outposts are closer but if you miscalculate you will be wandering in a huge expanse of trackless wilderness. Which should you choose? Without a second thought, strike out for Highway 105 directly west.

As mentioned in the signaling section, while you are walking out, try to stay ready to signal any airplane that might fly over. Airplanes fly regularly in many remote areas and might see you if you are in an open spot ready to signal.

Once you start moving, resist the temptation to rush towards your objective. Walk at a moderate or slow pace and stop long before dark to make camp. Keep safety foremost in mind. Never step over anything you can walk around, never step on anything you can step over. Be extremely careful crossing rivers and streams. If there isn't a safe crossing where you first encounter the river, follow it until you find one or make a raft. If you encounter an extremely large lake or river, people will probably come along sooner or later. Make camp and wait.

A river or chain-of-lakes is about the easiest highway to follow in winter when it is frozen over. The snow cover is usually much less on the ice than on the land, and of course, it offers a definite highway that eventually will lead somewhere. But, even in the far north ice can be treacherous. Swiftly running water, unseen from the top can cause the ice to be very thin over rapids or where the normal flow is compressed between two banks. A thick snow cover at the shoreline can insulate so well the water doesn't freeze very thickly. Sometimes it is impossible to tell if ice is thick enough to be safe by looking at it.

But, on the positive side, most ice in the north will hold up a man. You can usually tell if the ice is too thin by probing ahead of you with a sturdy stick. If you have a good knife along, lash it securely to a stick about four feet long and two inches thick. Keep jabbing the ice ahead of you as you walk. If the ice is too thin to hold you up, the knife blade will go through.

Some northwoods travelers carry a long, light weight pole with them while walking on the ice. The pole is held at the center so if you fall through it will keep you from going down under the ice. But, having participated in long treks over the ice, I know that after a day or two without any problems, most hikers will forget about the pole. It is too much trouble to carry. With no pole, your sheath knife is the best friend you have because if you fall through in a place where it is too deep to touch bottom, you might not be able to get back up on the ice again unless you have a hand hold.

If this happens, remove your sheath knife from its sheath very carefully so you don't drop it because your life might now depend on it. Grip it securely, hold yourself as far up on the ice as you can and then drive the point of the knife into the ice. Use this as an anchor point to pull yourself back up on the surface of the ice.

If the weather is cold so the snow is dry, roll immediately in the snow to remove as much water as you can from your clothing. Then get to shore and build a fire. If you can't build a fire, the only chance you have of surviving is to keep moving until your clothing dries out. Otherwise you will almost certainly die of hypothermia.

If you encounter a large river while walking out, follow the river. It will probably lead to help eventually. Moreover, you are very likely to encounter other people or see aircraft along a good sized river. Personally I would not try to walk any further unless I was sure that help was close by. I would either make a raft and float down the river or make camp and stay put until someone came along. But, like most other aspects of survival, this would be a judgement call.

Glaciers and large lake ice can have deep cracks filled with snow. If you fall in one, you might not get back out. About the only way to know if a snow filled crack is in your path is to keep probing the snow ahead with a pole. If it is summer and the glacier ice is melting, water will be running everywhere, even making ditches too deep to cross. Travel from midnight to midmorning if possible to avoid most of the running water. Snowslides are also a hazard to travelers in the far north in mountainous or glacier terrain. If you get caught in a snowslide, try to swim to the top as if you were swimming in water.

In winter and fall the desert might be a friendly place to travel. The temperature is agreeable and usually you can sight a distant landmark to keep oriented. A range of mountains in the distance, for instance, might be the only landmark you will need for days. The chief danger might be from flash floods or from the night actually getting so cold that you will suffer from hypothermia. Try to rest in a cave or depression out of the wind but high enough so a flash flood during the night will not catch you unaware.

Conversely, in the summer the desert becomes a hell hole, so hot and dry that a man can die without water if he tries to walk in the heat of the day. The best chance you have is to drink all the water you can, carry all that you can, and walk only during the cool part of the morning or late in the afternoon. The desert can be cooler after dark but you might fall over a cliff or even walk in a circle without the sun to guide you. If you happen to have a flashlight or if the moon is bright and you have a compass or trail to follow, night travel is an alternative.

Try not to walk in soft sand by traveling on ridges or troughs between dunes. Take good care of your feet by dumping sand out of your shoes regularly. If a sand storm comes up, lie down with your back to the wind and cover your face with a handkerchief or other cloth. If you get caught out in the open in the heat of the sun, dig into the sand as far as you can and cover your body with sand. This can keep you twenty degrees cooler than the ambient temperature.

8. GETTING OUT BY RIVER

If a river flows by your camp you have a ready-made route to follow out. Every river flows somewhere that help can be found. The river can be used as a carrier, so if possible make a raft.

Along almost every large stream or river you will find material for building a log raft. Sometimes only two logs are needed to make a raft. Unless you are far upstream from an unnavigable part of the river chances are the best thing you can do is make as comfortable camp as possible and wait for someone to come along. This probably will not take long in most areas as people are floating and motoring on every large river during the ice-free months. Some rivers are as busy as highways.

In some places, fallen but sound logs are strewn about in good numbers. Once you find the material for building the raft, reducing the logs to the right size is the next project. You will find the need to use smaller logs due to the weight of the larger ones. About the easiest way to build a raft is to lay the poles side by side and lay another smaller log across and tie them together with rope. If you do not have rope, the logs can be held together with notched stick.

Be sure to build the raft large enough to hold up everything you have as cargo. The bigger the better. Be sure to build the raft rectangular, rather than square as it will be easier to steer. Then you will need to build a deck over the first layer of logs so you can stay dry. Also, you will have to find or make a pole or sweep in order to steer the raft. Travel using the raft only when it is light enough to see ahead. Even then stay close to the shoreline so you can land in a hurry if noise ahead indicates rapids or gorges. Never enter unknown rapids without getting out and walking ahead and looking for danger. Usually you can line the raft through rapids by letting it down on a rope. Another possibility is to take it apart and let it float down one log at a time, or build another below the dangerous area. Of course you could also take the chance of letting it float through hoping it will make it, then catch it below the rapids.

Usually it will be quicker and safer to walk out than try to build a raft and float out. But there are clear exceptions. if you find a large stream or river with a good current but very little, if any, rapids or very shallow water and you have more than a hundred miles to go, then a raft might be feasible, especially if material for building the raft is close to the river.

APPENDIX 1

Surface-to-Air Emergency Signals

The traditional 18 International Surface-to-Air Emergency Signals were often not well known to pilots. So they recently have been replaced with five easily memorized signals by the International Convention on Civil Aviation:

  I require assistance

  I require medical assistance

N No

Yes

Proceeding in this direction

Air-to-Ground Signals consist of:

Will drop message: gun motor three times
Received message: rock plane, side to side
Affirmative: "nod" plane
Negative: "wag" plane
Fire or other location here: circle three times

APPENDIX 2

Basic Survival Kit

You should be careful when packing a survival kit. The temptation to over pack will be strong, so be careful to pack only the essentials needed in a survival situation. The list below is a good example of a sample basic survival kit.

_____ Waterproof matches

_____ Sturdy matches

_____ Fire starter

_____ Plastic whistle

_____ Signal mirror

_____ Card with Surface-to-Air signals

_____ Coins for a pay phone

_____ 1/8 inch nylon cord, 100 ft.

_____ Compass

_____ Flashlight

_____ Metal pot with bail

_____ Map

_____ Plastic or nylon tarp

_____ Toilet paper

_____ First aid kit

_____ Sunburn cream

_____ Folding saw

_____ Canteen, full

_____ Cup and spoon

_____ Sunglasses

_____ Lip salve

_____ Emergency food

_____ Water disinfection chemicals or filter

Optional: Fishhooks and line

APPENDIX 3

The Outdoor First Aid Kit

State-of-the-art dressings, wound closure tapes, and non-prescription medications allow the construction of a very useful first aid kit for general outdoor use.

Very often treatments can be improvised with other items on hand, but prior planning and the inclusion of these items in your kit will provide you with the best that modern medical science can offer.

This kit, and all of the individual components, are available from Indiana Camp Supply, as indicated below.

Quantity	Item
2 pkgs	Coverstrip Closures ¼" x 3" 3/pkg
1	Spenco 2nd Skin Dressing Kit
1	Bulb irrigating syringe
5 pkg	Nu-Gauze, high absorbent, sterile, 2 ply, 3" x 3" pkg/2
1	Surgipad, Sterile, 8" x 10"
2	Elastomull, Sterile Roller Gauze, 4" x 162"

2	Elastomull, Sterile Roller Gauze, 2½" x 162"
10	Coverlet Bandage Strips 1" x 3"
1	Tape, Hypoallergenic ½" x 10 YD
1	Hydrocortisone Cream .5%, 1 oz tube (allergic skin)
1	Triple Antibiotic Ointment, 1 oz tube (prevents infection)
1	Hibiclens Surgical Scrub, 4 oz (prevents infection)
1	Dibucaine Ointment 1%, 1 oz tube (local pain relief)
1	Tetrahydrozoline Ophthalmic Drops, (eye irritation)
1	Starr Otic Drops, ½ oz bottle (ear pain, wax)
1	Micronazole Cream, 2%, ½ oz tube (fungal infection)
24	Actifed Tablets (decongestant)
24	Mobigesic Tablets (pain, fever, inflammation)
24	Meclizine 25 mg tab (nausea, motion sickness prevention)
2	Ammonia Inhalants (stimulant)
24	Benadryl 25 mg cap (antihistamine)
10	Bisacodyl 5 mg (constipation)
25	Diasorb (diarrhea)
25	Dimacid (antacid)
2 pkg	Q-tips, sterile, 2 per package
1	Extractor Kit (snake bite, sting, wound care)
6	1 oz Vials for repackaging the above
1	Over-pak Container for above

Consideration should be given to a dental kit. Several are commercially available through backpacking and outdoor outfitters. As a minimum, a small bottle of oil of cloves can serve as a topical toothache treatment or a tube of toothache gel can be obtained. A fever thermometer should be included on trips. People wearing contact lenses should carry suction cup or rubber pincher device to aid in their removal. An adequate means of water purification must also be arranged.

Additional modules to this kit are described in detail in an ICS Book publication, *Wilderness Medicine* by William W. Forgey, some of which include prescription level medications. The above kit, and the advanced treatment modules, can be purchased pre-packed, and /or the individual items may be purchased separately from Indiana Camp Supply, Inc., PO Box 211, Hobart, Indiana 46342 — telephone (219) 947-2525.

Index